CULVERTON KIDS MYSTERY STORIES 2

Mystery at Wolf Rocks

BY

D.A. KREILEIN

xulon
PRESS

CULVERTON KIDS MYSTERY STORIES

The Tombstone Treasure Mystery
Mystery at Wolf Rocks

To Sheryl, Sandy, and Steve—
my sisters and brother in life and
in the Lord—
thank you for all your love and support
through the years!

"Keep it down to a dull roar!"

"Let us not lose heart in doing good,
for in due time we will reap
if we do not grow weary."
Galatians 6:9 (NASB)

INTRODUCTION

Most kids deliver newspapers or mow lawns to earn summer spending money. Not 11-year-old Jeffer, his younger sister Snoops, and their pal Dinkus Malone—they wanted to do something different and exciting. In their very first adventure, *The Tombstone Treasure Mystery*, the three members of Sneakers Detective Agency stumbled onto a long-forgotten clue on an old tombstone. They soon discovered that it was the first in a series of codes that would lead to a valuable treasure hidden by the late Josiah Whitley, one of Culverton's most respected citizens. As they worked together to crack the codes, they realized that they weren't the only ones searching for the treasure! The young sleuths' confrontations with a mysterious stranger and their longing for earthly riches landed them in more trouble than they bargained for. Through it all, they depended on the Lord for wisdom and courage and, in the end, realized that the best treasure of all is found in a relationship with Jesus Christ.

CHAPTER ONE

"I wonder where Dinkus is," said Jeffer as he buttered a second slice of toast. "He was supposed to be here ten minutes ago, wasn't he?"

"Yep," said Snoops. She picked up her spoon and chased the last few remaining Cheerios around her bowl. "Got 'em!" she said, gobbling them down. "What're we gonna do today, Jeffer?"

"I thought we'd head into town and check out the latest Nick McCane mystery at the bookstore." He broke off a small piece of toast and tossed it into the waiting mouth of Caleb, the Elliotts' yellow Labrador retriever. "Then we'll stop by Peerson's Pet Shop and pick up some of Caleb's favorite treats."

Upon hearing the word "treats", the dog's ears perked up and he barked.

"He thinks that's a great idea!" said Snoops.

"Me, too," said Jeffer. "If I were a dog, I'd get awfully tired of munching on that dry kibble all the time." They were interrupted by a loud knock on the back door. "That must be Dink."

"C'MON IN!" yelled Snoops. They heard the slap of the screen door as their best friend and neighbor, William "Dinkus" Malone, entered the sun-drenched kitchen.

"What kept ya so long?" said Jeffer.

"I was delayed," said Dinkus.

"By what?" asked Snoops.

"By a big ol' stack of buttermilk pancakes," said Dinkus as he rubbed his breakfast-filled belly.

"With butter and maple syrup slathered all over 'em?" asked Jeffer. Dinkus nodded. Jeffer stared at his pitiful slice of charred toast and sighed.

"Do you still wanna go to the bookstore?" asked Dinkus.

"You bet we do!" said Snoops, her green eyes flashing with excitement. "And the pet shop, too." She leaned forward and grabbed the box of Cheerios. She began stuffing handfuls of the dry cereal into the bib pocket of her denim overalls.

"What in the world are you doin', Snoops?" said Dinkus.

"It's for later... in case I get hungry."

Dinkus shook his blond head and said, "You're like a squirrel hoarding acorns for the winter!" He wondered if the little oaty o's would taste linty after being stored in a pocket all day long.

"Let's put this stuff away and hit the road," said Jeffer. He and Snoops cleared the breakfast table and the trio scooted out the back door with Caleb following. "Sorry, boy," said Jeffer to the dog, "but you have to stay here in the backyard."

Snoops knelt down and wrapped her scrawny arms around his tawny muscular neck. "Don't worry. We'll be back later... with your treats." Caleb wagged his tail so hard that he nearly toppled over. Jeffer latched the back fence gate behind them and they walked down the driveway, the pea-sized gravel crunching beneath their well-worn sneakers. The mid-summer air was already hot and thick like the steam rising from a boiling kettle of crawfish. The stillness of the morning was broken by the distant whirring of a lawn mower. The sweet aroma of freshly cut grass wafted across the street and tickled the children's noses. They breathed in deeply.

"Ahhhh," said Dinkus. "I love the smell of summertime!"

* * *

Their first stop was Miller's Book Shop on the corner of Main Street and Culverton Road. The front display windows faced the Culverton town square and were filled with all the latest arrivals from the publishing world.

"Look! There it is... right in front," said Dinkus, pressing his round face up against the once-clean glass.

"I can hardly wait to read it!" said Jeffer.

"How much does it cost?" asked Dinkus.

"Eight dollars and 95 cents," said Jeffer, "plus tax."

"*Tacks?*" said Snoops. "Why do we have to give them tacks?"

"No, not tacks like thumbtacks," said Jeffer. "Tax, t-a-x."

"What's a tax?" said Snoops.

"Extra money you have to pay whenever you buy somethin'," said Jeffer.

"Oh," said Snoops with a puzzled look on her 8-year-old face.

"So do we have enough or not?" said Dinkus. They scrounged around in their pockets and pooled their money. Jeffer and Dinkus tallied it up while Snoops held her breath in anticipation.

"Altogether we have 19 dollars and 93 cents!" said Jeffer. "More than enough… with plenty left over to get Caleb's treats."

"What are we waitin' for?" said Dinkus. He pushed against the heavy glass door and entered the shop with Jeffer and Snoops at his heels. Old wooden bookcases lined the walls and stretched from the carpeted floor to the high ceiling. A group of huge, over-stuffed chairs surrounded a low, round coffee table like a herd of elephants around a watering hole. The air was pungent with the odd combination of pipe tobacco and homemade sugar cookies.

"Well, if it isn't the three members of Sneakers Detective Agency!" said Mrs. Miller. "What can I do for you today?" Her voice and smile were as warm and welcoming as a mug of hot cocoa on a cold snowy night.

"We're here for the new Nick McCane mystery," said Jeffer as they crowded around the front counter.

"I've got one right here," said Mrs. Miller, reaching under the display case. "I knew you three mystery-lovers would want one, so I was holding it for you." She placed the book on the glass countertop. The familiar purple and black spine read "Nick McCane Mystery Stories #14 *The Black Swamp Mystery.*"

"Gee, thanks, Mrs. Miller," said Dinkus. "How much do we owe you?"

"Nine dollars and 58 cents."

After doing some quick subtraction in her head, Snoops said, "That's 63 cents in tacks—uh, I mean tax."

Jeffer laid all their grimy coins and wadded up dollar bills on the counter. After handing Mrs. Miller the exact amount, he stashed the remaining cash in his jeans pocket.

"Thanks, kids," said Mrs. Miller. "Enjoy your new book!"

"We will!" said Dinkus as they scurried out the door. They hung a left and then a left again onto Main Street. They passed Miss Marcie's Hair Palace and the Hef-T-Rama Hardware Store before crossing the street to Peerson's Pet Shop.

"Hi, Mr. Peerson," Jeffer called out to the bald, heavy-set man behind the counter. Milt Peerson was a long-time resident of Culverton and his pet store was a popular place in the downtown shopping district. The shop was filled with the smell of wood shavings, the never-ending squeak of hamster wheels, and an amazing array of animals including puppies, kittens, snakes, lizards, Guinea pigs, parrots and parakeets, tropical fish, rabbits, hedgehogs, rats and mice—and even monkeys!

"Good morning, Jeff," said Mr. Peerson. His bushy black mustache twitched slightly when he spoke, reminding the children of a furry caterpillar. "How's that Labrador of yours doing?"

"Caleb? He's doin' just fine," said Jeffer. "Growin' like a weed and eating us out of house and home... at least that's what Mom says!"

"So you named him Caleb?" said Mr. Peerson. "Did you know that 'Caleb' means 'dog'?"

"*What?*" said Snoops, glaring at Jeffer. "You mean we named our dog 'Dog'?"

"I guess so," said Jeffer sheepishly, "but I didn't know that. Besides, 'Caleb' also means 'bold'... and that suits him."

Snoops' attention quickly turned to a pen full of wriggling, squirming golden retriever puppies. "Jeffer! JEFFER!" she said. "Look at 'em. They're all so cute and fuzzy!" She giggled while three of them licked her freckled nose with their little pink tongues.

"It's The Attack of the Killer Furballs!" said Dinkus, his blue eyes twinkling with laughter.

"Sometimes I wish that puppies could just stay puppies," said Snoops, burying her face in a ball of golden fuzz. "That way they'd be cute and fluffy like this forever!"

"Are you looking for anything in particular today?" inquired Mr. Peerson.

"Yes, we need some of Caleb's favorite treats," said Jeffer, "those soft barbecue flavored jerky chips."

"They're in the second aisle, bottom shelf," said Mr. Peerson. "My nephew Tarp is over there stocking them right now."

"What kind of name is Tarp?" whispered Dinkus to Jeffer.

"I don't know," said Jeffer, "but I'm glad it's not mine!"

"Me, too," said Snoops, joining the boys. They wandered toward the second aisle, pausing to examine other items along the way.

"Dink, look at this," said Jeffer, holding up a shiny silver dog whistle.

"That is sharp," said Dinkus. "Let's see if it works." He placed the whistle between his lips and blew. A canine chorus of barks and howls and yelps and yaps flooded the store!

"I THINK IT WORKS!" said Jeffer loudly over the din.

"But I didn't hear anything," said Snoops, frowning.

"You're not supposed to," said Jeffer. "A dog whistle is so high-pitched that humans can't hear it... but dogs can." Snoops was not at all sure what good a whistle was that couldn't be heard.

"Let's get it," said Dinkus. "We have enough money for it *and* Caleb's treats with a little left over."

"OK," said Jeffer. They reached aisle two and spotted Tarp Wilbur, Mr. Peerson's 23-year-old nephew, unpacking a brown cardboard box.

"Hi, Tarp," said Jeffer. "Do you have any of the barbecue jerky chips?"

"Here," grunted Tarp as he handed Jeffer a bag. His mousy brown hair hung low over his eyes like a sheepdog in need of a trim.

"Thanks," said Jeffer.

The three children hurried to the register, paid for the treats and the dog whistle, and dashed out the door. When they got outside, Jeffer opened the bag, pulled out the whistle, and crammed it into his pocket.

"Can we go across the street?" said Snoops, fingering a shiny new dime that had been hiding in her back pocket. "I want to get a strawberry gumball out of the machine in front of the pharmacy."

"Sure," said Jeffer. "C'mon." They looked both ways and crossed Main Street.

A young red-haired boy stood in front of the drugstore window, his head hanging low. He glanced up with a worried look. A flash of recognition passed over his face and he said, "Aren't you guys those detectives that found the Whitley treasure?"

"Yes," said Jeffer. "I'm Jeff Elliott. This is Dinkus Malone and this here's my sister Snoops—uh, Rebecca."

"Sneakers Detective Agency at your service," Dinkus said proudly.

"I'm Josh," said the boy. "Are you taking on any new cases?"

"We sure are!" said Dinkus. "How can we help you?"

"My dog ran away," said Josh. "Can you help me find him?"

"A runaway dog?" whispered Dinkus to Jeffer and Snoops. "This really isn't the kind of case we had in mind, is it?"

"No," said Jeffer, "but it's not like we have any other business right now." Snoops and Dinkus nodded their heads. Jeffer turned to Josh and said, "We'd be happy to take you on as a client."

"How much do you charge?" asked Josh.

"Our rates are determined on a case-by-case basis," said Dinkus, trying to sound official.

"Case-by-case?" said Josh. "Well, in my case, I have no money. Could you still help me? Please?" His big brown eyes filled with tears as he pleaded with them.

"Well," said Jeffer thoughtfully, "I suppose we could take your case pro bono."

"Pro what-o?" said Snoops.

"Pro bono," said Jeffer, "meaning we would do it for free."

"For *free*?" said Josh. "That would be great... thank you!"

"You've been watchin' all those lawyer shows on TV again, haven't you?" mumbled Dinkus.

"Let's get started," said Jeffer, ignoring Dinkus' comment. "Dink, do you have your pen and notebook with you?"

"Sure do," said Dinkus, pulling them out of his back pocket. "I'll take down all the vital information." He uncapped the blue ballpoint pen and flipped open the notebook to a blank page. He quickly scrawled "Case No. 2" across the top.

"Josh, what's your dog's name?" asked Jeffer.

"Fuzzball."

"Fuzzball?" said Snoops.

"Yeah, Fuzzball," said Josh. "He's a Pomeranian... ginger-colored... and he looks like a giant ball of fuzz."

"When and where did you last see him?" said Jeffer.

"Half an hour ago... right here in front of Culverton Pharmacy," said Josh. "I tied his leash to this parking meter and when I came out, he was gone!"

Jeffer stooped down to inspect the leash that was lying limply on the sidewalk. It was still attached to the post of the gray metal meter. "Hm-m-m," he said, rubbing his chin.

"What is it?" said Snoops.

Jeffer straightened up, gazed at Josh, and said, "Fuzzball didn't run away... *he was stolen!*"

CHAPTER TWO

"**S**TOLEN?" said Josh. "How can you tell?"

Jeffer held up the end of Fuzzball's blue nylon leash and said, "It's been cut."

"Why would anyone want to steal Fuzzball?" cried Josh.

"I don't know," said Jeffer, shaking his head, "but we'll find out."

"That's right," said Dinkus. "If we can figure out *why* he was stolen, maybe we can figure out *who* stole him."

"Don't worry, Josh," said Snoops. "We'll do everything we can to find him."

"In the meantime," said Jeffer, "why don't you go on home and tell your folks? They can call Sheriff Logan and help you make some 'Missing Fuzzball' posters to distribute around town."

Josh wiped his dirty, tear-stained face with the back of his hand and said, "You mean like the other posters I've seen?"

"What other posters?" said Jeffer.

"The ones that are tacked up on the bulletin board."

"You mean the Culverton Community bulletin board over on the square?" said Dinkus.

"Yeah," said Josh, "it's full of 'em." Jeffer looked at Dinkus; Dinkus looked at Snoops; Snoops looked back at Jeffer.

"LET'S GO!" yelled Jeffer. He took off like a rocket from a launch pad with Snoops and Dinkus trailing behind. They shot down Main Street toward the town square.

"Wait for me!" said Snoops, trying desperately to keep up with the boys. When she finally caught up to them, they were leaning casually against the Civil War cannon that sat on the edge of the Culverton Village green.

"What took ya so long, Snoops?" said Dinkus. He stretched his arms and feigned a yawn. Jeffer chuckled.

"Very funny," said Snoops, scowling. "I can't help it if my legs are three years shorter than yours and Jeffer's."

"I know," said Dinkus, grinning. "I'm just kiddin' with ya."

"Let's check out those flyers," said Jeffer. "We've got a mystery to solve!" The three detectives huddled around the nearby bulletin board and scanned the content of the posters.

"Wow! Would you look at that!" said Dinkus. "The whole board is covered with missing dog flyers!" Jeffer shook his head in disbelief and Snoops' mouth hung open like the door flap on an old metal mailbox.

"I think our town has a serious problem," said Jeffer.

"I think you're right," said Dinkus. "It needs a bigger bulletin board!"

Jeffer jabbed him in the ribs with his elbow. "It's not funny. Just look at all these missing dogs!"

"Jeffer," said Snoops, "do you think they were stolen, too... like Fuzzball?"

"I don't know," said Jeffer, "but it's possible. For this many dogs to go missing at the same time is very suspicious."

"What're we gonna do?" said Snoops.

"First, we'll collect the information from these flyers and then we'll go see Sheriff Logan."

"Sounds like a good plan of action to me," said Dinkus, pulling out his notebook and pen. "Where should I start?"

"Start with the names of the dogs and what breeds they are," said Jeffer. "Can you write 'em down in columns?"

"Sure," said Dinkus. He drew some not very straight lines down the length of the paper and began scribbling feverishly, working his way from the right side of the board to the left.

"Are ya done yet?" said Snoops impatiently.

"Almost." After jotting down the details from the last two posters, Dinkus tucked the pen snugly behind his ear. "Now I'm done."

"Let's see it!" said Snoops, standing on the tip of her tippy tippy toes to get a better look.

NAME	BREED
Winston	Bulldog
Schultz	German Shepherd
Dempsey	Boxer
Horse	Great Dane
Oscar and Mayer	Dachshunds
Chops	Mastiff
Jaws	Rottweiler
Callie	Labrador
Rocky	Coonhound
Taco and Nacho	Chihuahuas
Binkie	Doberman Pinscher
Angus	Scottish Terrier
Ruffles	Cocker Spaniel
Missy and Melody	Beagles
Beauregard	Bloodhound
Shadow	Collie

And last, but not least:

Toodles and Doodles	Toy Poodles

"Don't forget to add Fuzzball to the list," said Jeffer.

"Fuzzball... Pomeranian," mumbled Dinkus as he added Josh's pilfered pooch to the surprisingly long list.

"Now what?" said Snoops. "We know the names and breeds of the missing dogs... but how does that help us?"

"I'm not sure yet," said Jeffer. "We need some more information."

"Most of the flyers include when and where the dogs were last seen," said Dinkus.

"You're right," said Jeffer. "Why don't you add a couple of columns and record those details, too?"

"OK," said Dinkus.

"I've got an idea," said Jeffer. "I'll be right back." He spun around and darted back down Main Street.

"Where are ya goin'?" Snoops called after him. He didn't answer, so she turned her attention back to the bulletin board.

As Dinkus finished recording the last detail in his notebook, Jeffer sprinted toward them, clutching a paper in his hand.

"What's that?" said Snoops, pointing to the scrunched-up paper.

"It's a map of Culverton," said Jeffer. "Y'know, one of those free ones next to the cash register at the pharmacy."

"Why do we need a map of Culverton?" said Snoops.

"I thought we could plot out the locations where the dogs were last seen."

"Great idea!" said Dinkus. "Maybe there's some kind of pattern."

"And that pattern," said Jeffer, "may tell us where the thief will strike next."

"You guys sure are smart," said Snoops. "I never would have thought of that."

"Don't worry, Snoops," said Jeffer. "When you're 11, you'll be just as smart as we are."

"Maybe even smarter," added Dinkus.

"Do you really think so?" said Snoops hopefully.

"Sure," said Jeffer. "We just have three more years of stuff crammed into our brains than you do."

"Why don't we go over there and work?" said Dinkus, pointing to a green wooden picnic table a short distance away. The trio trudged through the grass and sat down at the table beneath a sprawling oak tree.

"It sure feels good to get out of the hot sun," said Jeffer, mopping the sweat from his brow. His straight brown hair was matted to his damp forehead. He flattened out the crumpled map and began digging around in his front jeans pocket.

"What're ya doin'?" said Dinkus.

"I've got a stub of a pencil in here some- where," said Jeffer. "Here it is!" He proudly displayed the dark brown, 2-inch long, chewed-up writing implement.

"You call *that* a pencil?" said Snoops. "It looks like a mummified worm!"

"It'll do," said Jeffer.

"Are ya ready?" said Dinkus.

"Yep," said Jeffer with the pencil poised in mid-air. "Be sure to read off the locations in chronological order."

"Crayon or logical order?" said Snoops. "What are ya talkin' about?"

"That's chron-o-log-i-cal order," said Jeffer slowly. "It means the order in which things happened." Dinkus proceeded to read aloud the 18 addresses, allowing Jeffer time to locate them on the map and draw a star. Except for the last sighting of Fuzzball in front of the pharmacy, the stars on the map formed an almost complete circle.

"Look at that!" said Dinkus, tracing the arc on the map with his index finger. "The bandit is steadily working his way around town."

"But what about Fuzzball?" said Snoops.

"He probably swiped him, too," said Jeffer, "even though it wasn't planned. Poor little Fuzzball was sittin' there, minding his own doggie business, when the thief drove by, spotted him, and snatched him up!"

"Other than Fuzzball," said Dinkus, "all the other thefts seem to be well-planned. I wonder where he'll go next."

"I'm guessing that he'll strike somewhere in this area," said Jeffer, pointing to the map, "if he wants to complete the circle."

"What streets are we talking about?" said Dinkus.

Jeffer leaned in closer to inspect the small print on the map. "Culverton Road... where it intersects with Oak Grove Road."

"Wait a minute..." said Dinkus.

"THAT'S WHERE WE LIVE!" they all shouted at once.

"C'mon," said Dinkus. "We better go check on Caleb and Muttley!" Muttley was Dinkus' dog. He was not a mutt at all, but was, instead, a huge, purebred Irish wolf-hound who just happened to look quite "muttish".

"Your house is closer, Dink," said Jeffer. "Let's go there first." The children raced east on Culverton Road with Snoops bringing up the rear. They bounded up the front walk, burst through the front door, and landed in a heap in the foyer.

"MUTTLEY!" yelled Dinkus. "MUTTLEY! WHERE ARE YOU?" A gray-brown dog as big as a small pony galloped into the room and pounced on top of the child pile. "Muttley... you're here... you're safe," said Dinkus, relieved. He wrapped his arms around the giant pooch and gave him a big hug.

"You can hug him more later," said Jeffer. "Right now we've gotta find Caleb!" The three children untangled themselves, flew out the front door, and took off down Culverton Road again. They veered right onto Oak Grove and dashed down the Elliotts' gravel driveway toward the backyard.

"CALEB! CALEB!" Jeffer called. They reached the gate and stopped dead in their tracks. Snoops gasped in dismay. The gate was hanging wide open and Caleb was nowhere to be seen!

CHAPTER THREE

"**O**h, no!" cried Snoops. "Wh-where's C-C-Caleb?"

"He's been dognapped!" said Jeffer.

"What're we g-g-gonna do, Jeffer?" said Snoops, fighting back tears. "We've got to find him... we've just got to!"

Jeffer put his arm around her trembling shoulders, clenched his jaw, and said, "We'll find him."

"Yeah," said Dinkus, "nobody's gonna mess around with the dogs of *this* town and get away with it!" The loud revving of an engine and the ear-splitting screech of tires jerked their attention out to the street. A charcoal gray panel van swerved away from the curb and sped down Oak Grove Road, leaving black skid marks on the pavement and the foul odor of burnt rubber in their nostrils.

"That must be the thief!" yelled Jeffer. He and Dinkus bolted for the road and chased after the van, but they were no match for the speeding vehicle.

"We're losin' him!" said Dinkus.

"Get the license plate number, Dink!" said Jeffer. Dinkus shifted his legs into high gear, leaving Jeffer in his dust. He was gaining ground when the van accelerated rapidly and disappeared from sight. Dinkus collapsed to the pavement, gasping for air. He was still trying to catch his breath when Jeffer caught up to him.

"Are you all right?" asked Jeffer. Dinkus nodded. Jeffer gave him a hand and yanked him to his feet. "Did ya get it? Did ya get the plate number?"

"No," said Dinkus, shaking his head and still breathing heavily. "It was covered with mud."

"Probably on purpose," said Jeffer. "Let's head back to the house and tell my folks what happened."

* * *

Jeffer munched quietly on his bologna and Swiss cheese sandwich. He stole a sideways glance at his little sister. Snoops' head was bowed, her shoulder-length brown hair hiding her face. "You really oughta try to eat somethin', Snoops."

"I'm not hungry," she whispered.

"Neither am I, but we've got to keep up our strength so we can work at rescuing Caleb... and all the other dogs, too."

Snoops raised her head and gazed at Jeffer with her big green tear-filled eyes. "What if we don't find him, Jeffer? What if we never see him again?"

Jeffer shook his head. "I don't know, Snoops. But we can't let ourselves get stuck on that thought or we'll never crack this case."

"Do you think that God knows where Caleb is?" sniffled Snoops, brushing away a tear.

"I *know* He does," said Jeffer, "because He knows *everything*."

"So He can help us find him, right?" said Snoops.

"Absolutely!" said Jeffer. "We can't give up."

"Like that verse Pastor Luke talked about last week? The one about not losing heart?"

"Exactly like that!" said Jeffer.

"How does it go again?" asked Snoops.

"'Let us not lose heart in doing good, for in due time we will reap if we do not grow weary.'"

"OK," said Snoops. "I won't give up if you don't." She scarfed down half of her sandwich and drained her milk glass dry like a human Shop-Vac.

"Let's finish up, get our bikes and helmets out of the garage, and go meet Dinkus," said Jeffer.

* * *

Jeffer and Snoops pedaled their way to the corner, where Dinkus was waiting for them. He was straddling his metallic blue bike and adjusting the chin strap on his safety helmet.

"Are we gonna go see Sheriff Logan?" asked Dinkus.

"Yeah," said Jeffer. "My dad called him and told him we were coming."

"Does he know about all the other missing dogs?" said Dinkus.

"Yes," said Jeffer. "We can give him the details when we see him. Do you still have your notebook with all the information from the flyers?"

"It's right here," said Dinkus, patting his T-shirt pocket.

The three detectives hopped on their mountain bikes and rode west on Culverton Road. They crossed to the far side of the town square and stopped in front of City Hall. They were parking their bikes in the metal rack when Sheriff Logan pulled up in his police cruiser. Jim Logan was 52 and had been Culverton's sheriff for the past two decades. Too much time behind the desk and too many barbecued chicken wings had slowed him down a bit in the last few years, but he could still out-run a lazy low-life law-breaker when necessary!

"Hi, kids!" said the sheriff as he got out of the car.

"Hi, Sheriff!" said Jeffer, Snoops, and Dinkus.

Jim Logan motioned for them to come join him on a nearby bench. When they were settled, he said, "Your dad told me about Caleb. I'll certainly do everything I can to help you find him."

"He told you about all the other dogs, too, didn't he?" said Dinkus.

"Yes, he did," said Sheriff Logan, "and I'm mighty concerned about how many are missing."

"Twenty-three—counting Fuzzball and Caleb!" said Snoops.

Dinkus pulled out his notebook and uncapped his pen. "Caleb... Labrador Retriever," he said as he solemnly added Jeffer and Snoops' beloved pet to the list. "Sheriff," said Dinkus, "why would anyone want to steal all these dogs?"

"I've been giving that a lot of thought," said the sheriff. He took off his hat and wiped the sweat from his brow with a clean white handkerchief. "Given the particular dogs that have been stolen, I think that the thief either wants to resell them or, perhaps, breed them and sell the puppies."

"What is it about the dogs that makes you think that?" asked Snoops.

"Well," said Sheriff Logan, "they're all purebreds... not a mix or a mutt among them."

"And purebreds are worth more, aren't they?" said Jeffer.

"A lot more," said the sheriff.

"Wh-what if they s-s-sell Caleb?" said Snoops, her eyes wide with fright. "How will we ever find him?"

"Now, Rebecca," Sheriff Logan said, "let's not get ahead of ourselves. Caleb was snatched this morning... the dognapper is probably still in the area." His deep voice, calm as a lake on a windless summer day, comforted Snoops.

"Do you really think so?" said Snoops.

"Yes, I do."

"And we know what kind of vehicle he's driving," said Jeffer.

"A dark gray panel van," said Dinkus. "But we couldn't get the license plate number because it was covered with mud."

"That's interesting," said the sheriff. "Several other pet owners reported seeing the same vehicle in their neighborhoods when their dogs were taken."

"Did any of them see which way it went?" said Jeffer.

"Yes. Three of them observed it heading south on Main Street... out of town."

"Main Street turns into County Road 127, doesn't it?" asked Jeffer.

"It sure does," said the sheriff. "He could be hiding out somewhere along there. It's heavily wooded with a lot of houses and cabins out that way. Deputy Meeks and I have been patrolling in that area, hoping to catch sight of the van."

"We'll keep our eyes peeled, too," said Dinkus.

"Oo, yuck!" said Snoops. "Why would we want to peel our eyeballs?"

Jeffer chuckled and said, "It's just an expression, Snoops. It means 'to watch out for'." Snoops looked relieved.

Sheriff Logan stood up and put his hat back on his balding head. "You three will let me know if you see that van, won't you?"

"Yes, sir," said Jeffer, Snoops, and Dinkus. They watched as the sheriff got into his squad car and drove away.

"C'mon," said Jeffer as he took his lime green bike out of the rack. "Let's go!"

"Go where?" said Snoops.

"Down County Road 127, of course!" The young sleuths climbed on their bicycles like knights mounting their faithful steeds and headed south.

CHAPTER FOUR

"Can we take a break?" said Snoops. "My legs feel like they're made of concrete!" She steered her neon pink mountain bike onto the dirt shoulder of County Road 127. Jeffer and Dinkus joined her.

"We've been out here a long time," said Dinkus, using the bottom edge of his T-shirt to wipe the sweat from his face.

"And we haven't seen the van," added Snoops.

"I don't think we should give up yet," said Jeffer. "This is the best lead we've got on the dognapper." He paused to brush a few strands of hair out of his dark brown eyes. "If he's staying out here, he'll eventually *have* to come down this road."

"How 'bout we work our way back north," said Dinkus, "and stop at The Red Wolf Café for something cold to drink?"

"That sounds great!" said Snoops as she imagined doing a cannonball into a pool filled with fruit punch and giant ice cubes.

"I like that idea, Dink!" said Jeffer. "Let's go!"

The three worn-out detectives pedaled slowly toward the Culverton city limits and the waiting oasis. They explored every road and driveway that veered off to the right of County Road 127, hoping to spot the gray panel van. By the time they arrived at The Red Wolf Café, they were as tired as marathon runners at mile twenty-six.

The café was nestled in a shady hollow a quarter mile from where Howling Wolf Road intersected with County Road 127. The two-story log structure dated back at least 200 years. It had been a popular inn and tavern up until the late 1940's when it was restored and refurbished. Since then, it had been operating as a café, known for down-home cooking and a bottomless glass of sweet tea. Jeffer, Snoops, and Dinkus parked their bikes in the rack on the side of the building and trudged around front.

"Well, look what the cat dragged in!" called out Maggie McGregor as the trio hauled themselves through the doorway. Maggie had been the café's head waitress for as long as anyone in Culverton could remember! Her voice was low and rough like sandpaper from smoking too many cigarettes for too many years. Her hair, pulled back into a loose bun, was thinning and graying. A crisp white apron with two large pockets covered the front of her pink uniform dress and her plastic "My Name's Maggie" nametag tilted to the right.

"Hi, Maggie," said Jeffer.

"You kids look plumb tuckered out. Can I get you something cold to drink?"

"YES!" said Jeffer, Snoops, and Dinkus.

"Lemonades all around?"

"With lots of ice, please!" said Snoops. The children climbed onto three of the red vinyl-covered stools that surrounded the u-shaped counter.

"Hey, Pete!" yelled Maggie. "Look who's here!"

Pete Halverson poked his buzz-cut head through the opening between the dining room and kitchen and said, "It's my three favorite detectives!" A former navy man, Pete had been the short-order cook at the café since retiring from the military fifteen years ago. "What are you doin' way out here... workin' a case?"

"We sure are!" said Dinkus.

"There's a dognapper on the loose," said Jeffer, "and we're gonna catch him."

"He stole our Caleb," said Snoops quietly.

"And a bunch of other dogs, too!" said Dinkus.

"Sheriff Logan mentioned that when he was in here for a double bacon cheese-burger today," said Pete. "Anything we can do to help?"

"Yeah," said Jeffer, "keep an eye out for a dark gray van heading down 127. We've been out patrolling this afternoon, but haven't seen a thing."

"Will do!" said Pete, waving his greasy spatula in the air like a conductor's baton.

"Here you go, kids," said Maggie as she placed tall ice-cold glasses of lemonade in front of them. "On the house!"

"They're not on the house," said Snoops. "They're on the counter!"

Maggie's raspy laugh filled the café. "'On the house' means they're free, doll."

"Thanks, Maggie," said Jeffer. They each took a long, slow sip of the refreshing beverage.

"Ahhhhh," said Dinkus, "this is really hitting the spot!"

"What spot?" asked Snoops.

"The I-really-needed-a-cold-drink spot."

"Say," said Pete, sticking his head through the window again, "after you solve the dognapping mystery, I've got another one for you."

"Really?" said Dinkus. "What kind of mystery?"

"Do you kids know the legend of Wolf Rocks?" asked Pete.

"I've heard some things here and there," said Jeffer. "Somethin' about an old wolf living up there a long time ago."

"Let me tell you all about it," said Pete. He came out from the kitchen, wiping his beefy hands on his gravy-stained apron. He leaned on the counter, looked the children in the eyes, and said, "Long ago, when settlers first moved into this area, the Powhatan Indians shared with them The Legend of the Great Red Wolf. He was huge... 180 pounds of snarling, growling ferociousness."

"Ooooo, that's s-s-scary," said Snoops, her eyes as big as Frisbees.

"He was scary all right," said Pete. "He and his pack lived in a large cleft in Wolf Rocks."

"Red Wolf Cave, right?" said Jeffer.

"Right," said Pete. "To this day that cave is littered with deer bones and other animal skeletons left over from the pack's feasts. As more and more people settled in the area, deer became scarce. Old Red and his pack began attacking the settlers' sheep and cows. One dark and dreary night, a farmer shot and killed the Great Red Wolf. With their leader gone, the pack scattered... never to be seen again. Legend has it that, every so often, the ghost of Old Red can be seen high atop Wolf Rocks, mournfully howling at the moon."

"Has anyone s-s-seen him l-l-lately?" asked Snoops.

"That's just it," said Pete. "There hasn't been any wolf activity in these parts for 50 years or more. But—"

"Uh-oh," said Dinkus, shaking his head, "I knew there was gonna be a 'but'."

"But," continued Pete, "rumor has it that some of his descendants may have returned. There have been several reports of loud howling and one of our customers even saw a large wolf baying at the full moon a couple of months ago."

"I wonder if any of the wolves are as big as Old Red," said Jeffer.

"I don't know," said Pete, "but what I *do* know is that you kids should stay away from Wolf Rocks... at least for the time being."

"No problem," said Jeffer.

"Yeah, no problem," said Snoops.

"I have absolutely no desire to go any-where *near* the place," said Dinkus, "espe-cially if it means even the slightest pos-sibility of running into Old Dead Red's descendants!" Snoops and Jeffer nodded in whole-hearted agreement. They slurped down the last bit of tangy lemonade and hopped down from their stools.

"Thanks again for the drinks!" said Jeffer.

"You're welcome. Good luck finding the dognapper," Maggie called after them as they made a beeline for the door.

They rounded the corner of the building, yanked their bikes out of the rack, and climbed on. They turned north and began pedaling up a small rise in the road.

"Stay way to the right," said Jeffer. "I think I hear a car coming toward us... fast."

"If we can't see him, then he can't see us," said Dinkus.

"Let's pull off onto the shoulder and give him plenty of room... just in case," said Jeffer. They were standing by the side of the road when the speeding vehicle flew over the rise like a skier over a mogul.

"IT'S A GRAY VAN!" yelled Dinkus.

"Let's follow it!" said Jeffer. They spun their bikes around and rolled down the rise.

"We'll never be able to keep up!" said Snoops.

"Maybe not," said Jeffer, "but we might be able to see where it turns off."

"We're losin' it!" said Dinkus.

"It's turning right onto Morton's Gap Road," said Snoops.

"That's a break for us," said Jeffer. "There are only a few cabins back in there."

"Unless he's going all the way through the gap to Shadow Lake," said Dinkus.

"Let's hope not," said Snoops. "I don't think I can pedal that far."

"Either way," said Jeffer, "it works in our favor. He's off 127... the rutted back roads will slow him way down."

"And our mountain bikes will help us catch up!" said Dinkus. They made the turn onto Morton's Gap Road, their legs churning as fast as the blades of a blender set on purée. The old dirt road was narrow and wound its way through the dense woods and thick undergrowth.

"There it is!" said Jeffer, pointing ahead.

"He's turning right," said Dinkus. "There must be a cabin back in there."

Jeffer slowed down and said, "Don't get too close... we don't want him to see us." They turned right and coasted silently down a small hill. The gray van was parked beside a log cabin in a sunlit clearing. "Over there," whispered Jeffer, motioning to the woods on his left. "We can hide behind that big boulder." The three detectives concealed themselves and their bicycles behind the massive rock.

"I hear voices," said Jeffer. "An old guy and a young guy... but I can't understand what they're saying."

"I hear barking!" said Snoops.

"Me, too!" said Dinkus.

"We've gotta get closer," said Jeffer.

"How 'bout we belly crawl up to that fallen tree?" said Snoops.

"Good idea," said Jeffer. "C'mon!" They dropped to the ground and wriggled their way forward like short-legged lizards. They pulled themselves up behind the large decaying tree trunk and peered out over the top. Both men had their backs toward the youngsters as they began unloading bags and boxes from the back of the van. A black and white border collie was bounding around excitedly, glad to be free from the confines of the vehicle.

"Down, boy!" said the driver. "David, down!"

"The dog's name is David?" said Dinkus. "That's weird!"

"I've only ever known one guy whose dog was named David," said Jeffer.

"Who?" asked Snoops.

"Ralph Gorman."

"Who's Ralph Gorman?" said Snoops.

"He delivers groceries for the Grab-Yer-Grub Grocery Store in town... the one across the street from Miller's Book Shop," said Jeffer.

"David doesn't happen to be a border collie, does he?" said Dinkus slowly.

"Yep," said Jeffer.

"Does Ralph drive a gray van when he's making deliveries?" said Dinkus.

"Yep."

"Oh, man!" whined Dinkus. "We've been following a delivery boy!"

"A delivery boy?" said Snoops. "What a waste of time!"

"And energy," added Jeffer. "I don't know about you two, but all this ridin' around has worn me out."

"Me, too," said Snoops.

"Me, three," chimed in Dinkus.

"It's getting late," said Jeffer. "We better get home for dinner before our folks start worryin' about us."

As they pushed their bikes out of the woods and onto the dirt driveway, a long chilling howl sliced through the air like a meat cleaver through a pound of ground chuck. "OW-OW-OWOOOOOO!" Snoops screamed. Jeffer and Dinkus flinched. The hair on the back of all their necks stood straight up.

"It's the great, great, great grandson of Old Dead Red!" said Dinkus.

"LET'S GET OUTTA HERE!" yelled Jeffer.

CHAPTER FIVE

"There's nothing f-f-furry and f-f-ferocious f-f-following us, is there?" said Dinkus, fear creeping into his voice and causing it to tremble.

"Not that I can see," said Jeffer, nervously glancing back over his right shoulder. The three detectives pedaled furiously until they reached Oak Grove Road and the safety of the Elliotts' garage. They dismounted their bikes, flipped the kickstands down, and removed their helmets.

"Whew! That was way too close," said Dinkus, running his fingers through his sweaty blond hair.

"I'll say," said Jeffer. "That wolf must have been a stone's throw from the cabin!"

"And if you throw like I do," said Snoops, "then it wasn't v-v-very f-far at all!" She was still breathing heavily and her heart was pounding like a jackhammer on a block of cement.

"Scared out of our skins," said Dinkus, "and for what?"

"For nothin'!" said Jeffer as he tossed his helmet into a cobweb-filled corner of the garage. "I can't believe our prime suspect ended up being Ralph Gorman in the Grab-Yer-Grub delivery van!"

"What're we gonna do now?" said Snoops. "We're no closer to rescuing Caleb and the other dogs than we were this morning!"

"It *has* been a really long day, hasn't it?" sighed Jeffer.

"Yeah," said Dinkus, "and it's about to get even longer."

"What are ya talkin' about, Dink?" said Jeffer.

"I've got an idea... if you're both up for sleepin' in the tree house tonight."

"We're always up for that," said Jeffer.

"Yeah!" said Snoops.

"How 'bout we meet back here after supper... say 8:00?" said Dinkus.

"Sounds good," said Jeffer. "Do we need to bring anything special?"

"Nope... just the usual overnight stuff."

"Including homemade cookies?" said Snoops.

"Of course!" said Dinkus. "What's a campout without some of your mom's famous chocolate chip cookies?"

"All right," said Jeffer. "We'll see ya back here in a couple of hours... snacks and all."

* * *

"Hey, Snoops!" said Jeffer. "Would ya give me a hand out here with all this gear?"

"Sure," said Snoops. She pushed open the squeaky screen door and stepped out onto the back porch.

"Let's not forget this," said Jeffer, tossing *Nick McCane and the Black Swamp Mystery* onto the growing heap. "I thought maybe we could read some of it tonight."

"Or these," said Snoops, grinning and holding up a clear plastic zip-bag full of still-warm-from-the-oven chocolate chip cookies. They loaded the sleeping bags, pillows, flashlights, book, cookies, and canteens onto an old red wagon and began hauling it out to the big oak in the Elliotts' backyard. The wobbly wheels bumped over the knobby tree roots that stuck up out of the dirt and the children struggled to keep the pile upright in the wagon bed.

"We're almost there!" said Jeffer. "Only a few more feet to go." He parked the wagon next to the gnarled trunk of the enormous oak tree that supported their tree house.

Actually, the words "tree house" did not even begin to describe it. With three floors and a crow's nest, it was more like a "tree mansion"! A retractable rope ladder led the way up to the first floor, which was a large wooden deck surrounded by a two-foot high railing. The second floor was an enclosed room, which was entered by a trap door in the floor. It was constructed of plywood sheets and there were no windows, so the interior of the room was shielded from the weather. This was where Sneakers Detective Agency convened their secret meetings and stored all their "detectivating" equipment, assorted collections, and the ever-present three-pound jar of peanut butter (smooth, not chunky)... with crackers. A hatch in the ceiling opened up to a short section of wooden rungs. This allowed access to the third level, which was another plank deck with a railing. A large green canvas tarp was draped above this floor, offering limited protection from the sun and rain. The crow's nest, made from half a barrel, was reached by scaling a wide section of ship's rigging. A small, wooden flagpole and a telescope, both clamped to the barrel rim, topped it off. Other amenities in the "tree mansion" included an intricate rope and pulley system for hauling up supplies, over-sized slingshots attached to the first and third floor railings (with accompanying buckets of dirt-clod ammunition), a sunken hollow in the lower part of the trunk used as a mailbox, and a tire swing.

"I'll load the crate," said Jeffer, "and you can haul it up."

Snoops scampered up the ladder and grabbed hold of the rope hanging down from the pulley. "Ready?" she asked.

"Take it away!" said Jeffer, giving a thumbs up.

Snoops tugged on the rope and the over-flowing crate gradually rose into the air. The yellow nylon cord began slipping through her small hands. "It's really heavy, Jeffer."

"Hold on! I'll come help you." He quickly scaled the ladder and joined Snoops on the first floor. Together they hoisted up the wooden box and poured the contents out onto the deck.

"Go ahead and lower it back down," said Jeffer. "Dinkus'll need it for his stuff when he gets here."

"He should have been here by now," said Snoops. "I'm gonna go up top and keep an eye out for him." She scurried up the ladders and rigging like a seasoned sailor on the seven seas. Perched in the crow's nest, she aimed the telescope in the direction of the Malone house and peered through the eyepiece.

"Do ya see him?" said Jeffer.

"Not yet," said Snoops. "Wait a minute... I see someone. DINK AHOY!"

"Dink ahoy?"

"Yeah, Dink ahoy," said Snoops. She put her eye to the telescope again. "MUTTLEY AHOY!"

"Muttley ahoy?"

"Can't ya hear or somethin'?" said Snoops.

"I can hear just fine," said Jeffer. "I'm just wondering why he's bringing Muttley with him."

Dinkus plowed his way through the thick azalea hedge surrounding the Elliotts' backyard. His arms were loaded with his gear and he was pulling a reluctant Muttley along behind him. "Hi, guys," he said when he reached the back fence gate. By this time, Snoops had rejoined Jeffer on the first floor.

"Hi," said Jeffer. "What's with Muttley?"

"He's part of the plan," said Dinkus as he stuffed his gear into the crate.

"What exactly *is* the plan?" asked Jeffer.

67

"The plan is to use Muttley as bait for the dognapper."

Snoops gasped. "No, Dinkus, no! I don't think I could stand it if we lost Muttley, too!"

"She's right," said Jeffer. "It's too risky, Dink."

"It can work," said Dinkus. "I've thought it through."

"Yeah?" said Jeffer. "What are the details?"

"No, Jeffer! Don't encourage him," pleaded Snoops.

Dinkus continued, ignoring Snoops' plea for sanity. "We leave Muttley down here, at the base of the tree. We'll all be up on the first floor with this." He rooted around in his backpack and pulled out an old fishing net. "When the thief comes to grab Muttley, we drop the net on him!"

"Hm-m-m," said Jeffer, rubbing his chin. "I like it!"

"No, no, NO!" said Snoops, stomping her foot like a bull preparing to charge.

"This can work, Snoops," said Dinkus.

"I agree," said Jeffer. "We can protect Muttley, catch the dognapper, and get Caleb back!"

"NO!" said Snoops. Realizing that she was fighting a losing battle, she shook her head and said, "You guys are gonna do this no matter what I say, aren't you?"

"Yep," said Dinkus and Jeffer.

"Well, then," said Snoops, defiantly crossing her arms, "I just wanna say that I have a *really* bad feeling about this."

"Duly noted," said Dinkus. Using Muttley's long leather leash, he secured the hairy beast to one of the gnarly roots beneath the tree. He climbed up the rope ladder while Jeffer hauled up the crate.

"Hey, Dink," said Jeffer, "could you pull up the ladder after you? We don't want any uninvited company tonight."

"Like the dognapper," said Snoops.

"Or Old Dead Red and his descendants!" said Dinkus as he hauled it up.

"Thanks a lot, Dinkus," said Snoops, rolling her eyeballs. "I had almost forgotten about them!"

"OW-OW-OWOOOOOOO!" howled Jeffer.

" O W - O W - O W O O O O O O O ! " howled Dinkus.

"C'mon, Snoops!" said Jeffer.

Snoops threw her head back and joined the boys for one last howl. "OW-OW-OWOOOOOOOO!"

* * *

"These cookies are *so* good!" said Dinkus, reaching into the bag for a second one. They had spread out their sleeping bags and were sitting cross-legged in a circle around the snack supply: peanuts in the shell, apple wedges, spray cheese on crackers, and, of course, the chocolate chip cookies.

Snoops licked sweet gooey chocolate from her fingers and said, "Too bad we don't have any milk to dunk 'em in." She picked up the cheese can and sprayed some of the rubbery "cheese product" into her mouth. She squished it between her tongue and the roof of her mouth, forgetting about her missing front teeth until orange goo squirted out.

"Yuck! Snoops!" yelled Jeffer. "That's disgusting!"

"Sorry!" said Snoops. "I forgot about the hole where my teeth used to be!" She swallowed the remaining "cheese" and dabbed her mouth and chin with a paper towel. She stared at the hole in her left sneaker toe for several minutes before saying quietly, "Jeffer, I miss Caleb."

"Me, too."

"Do you think he misses *us*?"

Jeffer thought for a moment and said, "Yes, I do. He's been our Caleb since he was a little puppy and we're the only family he knows."

"Do you think he's all right?" asked Snoops.

"Yeah, I think he is."

"How do you know?" said Snoops.

"Remember how Sheriff Logan told us that the dognapper probably wants to sell or breed the dogs?"

"Yeah?" said Snoops.

"Well," said Jeffer, "if he wants to sell or breed them, he would have to take care of them."

"That's right!" said Dinkus.

"Does God care about Caleb and what happens to him?" said Snoops. "I mean, he is just a dog, not a person."

"Of course He does!" said Jeffer.

"Yeah!" said Dinkus. "Don't you remember that verse... the one about God knowing how hairy our heads are and how he takes care of the birds?"

"That sounds vaguely familiar," said Snoops.

"So, if God cares about birds, then he certainly must care about dogs," said Dinkus. "And if God knows how many hairs are on *our* heads, then He also knows how many hairs are on Caleb's whole body!"

"That's a lot of hair, Snoops!" said Jeffer.

"If He knows about every single strand of fur on Caleb, then he must care an awful lot about him," said Dinkus.

"I see what you mean," said Snoops. "I think he'll be OK until we can find him."

"And let's hope and pray that that is real soon," said Jeffer.

"It will be if my plan works," said Dinkus.

"Are you sure Muttley is still down there?" said Snoops. "He's being awfully quiet."

"The dognapper won't strike until it's dark, but I'll check," said Dinkus. "MUTTLEY? YOU DOWN THERE?"

"ARF! ARF!"

"He's still there."

Jeffer wiped his cheesy fingers on his jeans and said, "How 'bout I read some of *The Black Swamp Mystery* while we wait for it to get dark?"

"Great idea!" said Dinkus, snatching another cookie out of the bag.

"I hope it's not too scary," said Snoops. "I've had enough of that for one day." She fluffed up her pillow and snuggled down into her sleeping bag.

"Don't worry, Snoops," said Jeffer, "me and Dinkus will protect you." He cracked open the book and began reading. The slowly setting sun and the drone of Jeffer's voice made Snoops' eyelids heavy.

"Hey, Snoops," said Dinkus, "if you want to sleep a little, Jeffer and I can take the first watch. OK?"

"Yeah, sure," mumbled Snoops. The last thing she remembered was Nick McCane wading hip-deep into the brackish waters of Black Swamp.

* * *

The early morning sunlight filtered down through the bright green tree leaves and onto Snoops' freckled face. She yawned, stretched, and slowly opened her eyes. A robin, perched on a nearby branch, chortled cheerfully to its mate higher up in the tree.

Snoops rubbed the crusties from her eyes and said, "Hey, guys... thanks for letting me sleep all night. Too bad the dognapper never showed up." She waited for a response from her fellow campers. "Jeffer? Dinkus?" She stretched again and rolled over onto her stomach so she could talk to the boys. But the boys couldn't talk... THEY WERE SOUND ASLEEP!

CHAPTER SIX

"JEFFER! DINKUS!" yelled Snoops. The boys didn't move a muscle. They were like stone statues... except they were snoring! Snoops shook them and screamed at the top of her lungs, "WAKE UP! WAKE UP!"

"Stop yelling," mumbled Dinkus. "I'm tryin' to sleep."

"Me, too," said Jeffer groggily.

"YOU'RE NOT SUPPOSED TO BE SLEEPING!" hollered Snoops. "YOU'RE SUPPOSED TO BE CATCHING THE DOGNAPPER!" Her piercing screams finally penetrated their near-comatose brains. The boys sat bolt upright, eyed each other, and then gawked at a panic-stricken Snoops.

"OH, NO!" said Dinkus. He leaned over the railing and called, "MUTTLEY! MUTTLEY!"

There was no answer. Before Jeffer and Snoops could stop him, he leapt off of the deck to the hard ground ten feet below.

"Dinkus!" shrieked Snoops, fearing for her friend's safety. Jeffer lowered the rope ladder and he and Snoops scrambled down to join Dinkus on the ground.

The down-cast expression on Dinkus' face said it all. He was holding the freshly cut end of Muttley's leash and staring at the ground. "He's gone. He's really gone," said Dinkus quietly.

"Don't worry, Dink," said Jeffer. "We'll find Muttley... and Caleb."

Dinkus was fighting back tears and losing the battle. "Snoops was right... it was a dumb idea. We shouldn't have risked Muttley. I've only made things worse."

Jeffer put his hand on his best friend's shoulder and said, "It's gonna be all right, Dink."

"We'll find 'em," said Snoops, "because we're not gonna stop searching 'til we do!"

* * *

After a hearty breakfast of sunny-side-up eggs, sizzling bacon, and cold orange juice, the three members of Sneakers Detective Agency retreated to the second floor of the tree house.

"I think we need to have a strategy meeting," said Dinkus.

"Yeah," said Snoops, "a tragedy meeting."

Jeffer chuckled and said, "Not a *tragedy* meeting, Snoops... a *strategy* meeting."

"What kind of meeting is that?" asked Snoops.

"A meeting where we discuss our plan," said Dinkus.

"Do we *have* a plan?" said Snoops.

"Maybe," said Jeffer, rubbing his chin.

Snoops leaned over and whispered to Dinkus, "I think he's got an idea!"

"Well?" said Dinkus.

Jeffer leaned back in his chair, laced his fingers, and put his hands behind his head. He stared up at the rough plywood ceiling, deep in thought. "Hm-m-m...."

"You can almost hear the gears turning in his head, can't ya?" said Dinkus.

Snoops cocked her head to one side and listened intently. "I don't hear a thing," she whispered. Dinkus laughed.

"OK, how 'bout this for a plan?" said Jeffer. Dinkus and Snoops craned their necks forward, anxious to hear his newly-hatched scheme. "There are three of us, right?"

"Last time I counted," said Dinkus.

"Instead of staying together," said Jeffer, "we're gonna split up so we can cover more territory."

"That's a good idea," said Snoops.

"Dinkus, you and Snoops will stay here in town and stake out two different areas. You'll try to catch the dognapper in the act... or at least spot the van."

"What about you?" said Dinkus.

"I'll be stationed outside The Red Wolf Café. If the thief heads out of town down 127, I'll follow him."

"How will you know if he's headed your way?" asked Dinkus.

"Ahhhh," said Jeffer, holding his right index finger up in the air. "Let me show you." He removed a large plastic bin from the bottom of one of the cinder block and board shelves that lined two of the walls. He dragged it across the floor, pried off the lid, and began rummaging through the newspaper-wrapped contents.

"What're ya lookin' for, Jeffer?" said Snoops.

"Dad's old walkie-talkies."

"Walkie-whaties?" said Dinkus.

"Walkie-*talkies*," said Jeffer. "I know they're in here somewhere." He clawed through the items like a packrat digging a deep burrow. "Here they are!" he said, holding up three rectangular-shaped objects. Each of the outdated hand-held radios was yellow and black with a red button on one side, an on/off switch, and a 12-inch antenna sticking out of the top.

"These are walkie-talkies?" said Dinkus.

"Yep," said Jeffer.

"What do they do?" said Snoops, cautiously eyeing the strange objects.

"Think of them as antique cell phones," said Jeffer.

"Did people really use these before there were cell phones?" said Dinkus.

"All the time."

"Why don't we just use cell phones?" said Snoops.

"Yeah, why don't we?" said Dinkus.

Jeffer scowled at Snoops and Dinkus. "Do any of us *have* our own cell phones?" They shook their heads "no" in unison like bobble headed dogs in a car's rear window. "That's right... the answer is a big, fat 'NO'! As private eyes we might be a little technologically challenged, but these walkie-talkies are the next best thing. All we need are some fresh batteries and we're good to go!"

* * *

"Testing... testing... 1-2-3," said Jeffer into his walkie-talkie.

"I don't hear anything," said Snoops. "Are you sure these old things even work?"

"Did you turn it on?" asked Jeffer smugly.

"Oops... sorry." She flicked the switch to "ON" and heard a low level of static coming out of the miniature speaker. "Try it now."

"Testing... testing... 1-2-3," repeated Jeffer.

"I heard you that time! I heard you!" said Snoops, her green eyes lighting up like sparklers on the 4th of July.

"Me, too!" said Dinkus.

"Now try saying something into it," said Jeffer. "When you want to talk, just push in that red button on the side."

Snoops pressed the button and said, "Testing... testing... 1-2-3."

"Loud and clear," said Jeffer. "Now you try, Dink."

"Testing... testing... 1-2-3."

"You're loud and clear, too," said Jeffer. "A couple of things to remember—when you're done talking, say 'Over' and then release the button so you can hear us answer back. And if you want to say 'Yes' or 'OK', say '10-4' or 'Roger' instead."

"Who's Roger?" asked Snoops.

Jeffer grinned and said, "Roger's not a person, Snoops. It's just a word."

"Why Roger?" said Dinkus. "Why not Floyd or Herman?"

"I don't know!" said Jeffer, getting a little irritated. "That's what they say on all the old cop shows."

Dinkus shrugged his shoulders and said, "That's good enough for me!"

"Now for our assignments," said Jeffer. He leaned over the orange-crate table and studied the map of Culverton. "Dinkus, why don't you head on over to the town square?"

"That's a great location," said Dinkus. "To go to or from almost anywhere in town, you have to pass through there."

"What about me?" said Snoops.

Jeffer glanced at the map again and said, "You're going to be posted at the intersection of Oak Grove Road and Willowdale Avenue."

"Is that where the school is?" said Snoops.

"Yes. And I'll head down to the café here," said Jeffer, pointing to the map.

"Are you sure you'll be able to hear us on our walkie-talkies that far away?" said Dinkus.

"They've got a range of about a mile, so we should be all right." Jeffer wadded up the map and stuffed it in his T-shirt pocket. "I guess we're all set."

"What're we waitin' for?" said Dinkus. "Let's get this stake-out started!"

* * *

"Jeffer, Snoops, can you hear me?" said Dinkus. "I'm by the cannon on the village green. Over."

"You're loud and clear," said Jeffer. "I'm still riding south on 127. I should be at The Red Wolf Café in about five minutes. Snoops, you out there? Over."

"I'm here at the school. Over."

"Let's stay alert and keep our eyes open for that van," said Jeffer.

"You forgot to say 'Over.' Over," said Snoops. She knew she was being a smart-aleck, but she said it anyway.

Jeffer rolled his eyeballs, took a deep breath, exhaled, and reluctantly said, "Over."

* * *

The sweltering hot summer morning stretched into an even hotter summer afternoon. The three detectives doggedly stuck to their posts, waiting anxiously for a break in the case.

"Jeffer," whined Snoops, "I'm hungry. Over."

"Me, too, Snoops. We probably should have packed some sandwiches. Over."

"Please don't say the word 'sandwiches'. It just makes me hungrier," said Snoops. "Over."

"Hey!" said Dinkus. "Did you forget about the Cheerios you squirreled away in your pocket yesterday morning? Why don't you munch on a few of those? Maybe that'll help you hang in there a while longer. Over."

"Oh, yeah! Thanks for reminding me. Over," said Snoops. She unsnapped the bib pocket on her overalls and peered inside.

Surprisingly, most of the little oaty o's were still intact! The remains of a few crushed ones formed a thin layer of oat dust in the bottom of her pocket. She was about to toss a handful of the cereal into her mouth when something across the street caught her eye. She crammed the cereal back into her pocket and snapped it shut.

"Jeffer! Dinkus! I've spotted a gray van! Over."

"Where is it? Over," said Dinkus.

"Across the street at the Nibbles and Nozzles gas station on the corner of Oak Grove and Willowdale," said Snoops. "I'm gonna go over there and investigate. Over."

"OK," said Jeffer. "Let's not get too excited just yet. It might be Ralph Gorman and the Grab-Yer-Grub delivery van again. Over."

"All right," said Snoops. "Give me a few minutes and I'll report back. Over." She pushed her walkie-talkie down deep into one of the side pockets of her overalls and jogged across the street. The van was parked on the left-hand side of the building and the driver was nowhere in sight. *He must be inside buying something*, Snoops said to herself. *Perfect... it'll give me a chance to check out the van!* She scampered across the hot asphalt like butter dancing across a sizzling skillet.

"ARF! ARF!"

"Barking!" said Snoops. "Maybe it's Muttley. I've got to get a look inside!" She stepped up onto the black rubber bumper and peeked through a small open window in the rear door. Wire cages were stacked up on both sides of the cargo space and they were filled with dogs! She frantically searched the rows of cages for some familiar furry faces. She was not disappointed. "MUTTLEY! CALEB! AND FUZZBALL, TOO! I've got to tell the boys." She pulled out her walkie-talkie, pressed the red button, and said, "Jeffer! Dinkus! Come in! Over."

"I'm here. Over," said Dinkus.

"Me, too. What's goin' on, Snoops? Over," said Jeffer.

"You'll never believe it!" said Snoops. "The van is full of dogs... including Caleb, Muttley, and even Fuzzball!" She heard the boys cheering through the slight static. "What should I do, Jeffer?"

"Wait right there. Dink, you're only a couple of blocks away. Get over there as fast as you can! Over."

"10-4," said Dinkus. "I'm on my way, Snoops! Over."

Snoops sat down on the bumper to wait for Dinkus. She took a few deep breaths, trying to calm her racing heart. The bell on the gas station door jingled and Snoops wondered, *Did someone go in...or did someone come out?* The driver's side door of the van slammed shut and the radio's volume was cranked up to the max. "What am I going to do? WH-WHAT AM I GOING TO D-D-DO?" Snoops' heart was beating wildly and she could barely breathe. "I've got to stay with the d-d-dogs... I've just g-g-got to!"

She climbed back up on the bumper, grabbed hold of the open window frame, and pulled herself up. Her head and shoulders were through when she felt the vibration of the revving engine. The van backed up with a screech, propelling her through the window and onto the hard steel floor of the cargo area! The vehicle lurched to a stop at the edge of the parking lot, causing Snoops to slide forward and slam into the metal wall that divided the cab from the cargo space.

"OW!" she cried. She grabbed her right elbow and felt a warm trickle of blood run over her fingers. "Yuck!" She wiped the blood on her overalls and crawled back to the door. She pulled herself to her feet and gazed out the window just in time to see Dinkus arriving on his bike. She waved frantically and called out, "DINKUS! DINKUS!"

Dinkus looked up and caught a glimpse of Snoops' ghost-white face poking out through the window of the dognapper's get-away vehicle! "SNOOPS!"

CHAPTER SEVEN

T he van's black rubber tires squealed as it sped out of the Nibbles and Nozzles parking lot. It turned right and raced south on Oak Grove Road.

"DINKUS! DINKUS!" Snoops yelled, her head still hanging out of the rear window. "HELP!" She reached for her walkie-talkie with trembling hands and yanked it out of her pocket... in pieces! "Oh, no!" said Snoops. "It must have broken when I tumbled into the van." She nervously bit her lower lip as one lone tear rolled down her flushed cheek. "Dear Lord, wh-wh-what was I th-th-thinking when I crawled in here?" Snoops knew the answer even before she finished asking the question... she hadn't thought at all!

Dinkus was pedaling as fast as a washing machine on the spin cycle. "SNOOPS!" The vehicle swerved, veering right onto Fair Haven Street. Dinkus made up some ground when it slowed down to make the turn. He could see Snoops' face in the window. Her eyes were as big as pancakes and her mouth was hanging open. A block later the van turned left and headed down Route 127. It picked up speed on the country road and Dinkus struggled to keep it in view.

"Jeffer! Jeffer! Come in, Jeffer! This is Dinkus. We've got a situation. Over."

"Jeffer here. What sort of situation? Over."

"The van is headed your way... with Snoops inside!"

"WHAT?" said Jeffer. "How in the world did *that* happen?"

"Before I could get to the gas station, the dognapper came out, got in the van, and started the engine," said Dinkus. "The rear window was open and Snoops climbed in just as it tore out of the parking lot!"

"Why would she do that?"

"I guess she didn't wanna leave Caleb and Muttley once she found 'em."

"Dink, this is bad," said Jeffer, "*really, really* bad. What's gonna happen once the van gets to where it's going? What'll the dognapper do when he finds Snoops?"

"I don't know, Jeffer. Maybe she'll be able to climb out before then."

"I hope so," said Jeffer. "We've gotta make sure we keep the van in sight!"

"Get ready! It should be comin' around the curve and down the rise any second now."

"Snoops! Come in, Snoops! Over." The only reply he received was the steady crackle of static. Jeffer decided to start pedaling his bike down 127, hoping to cover some distance before the vehicle passed him. He heard the eardrum-piercing blast of the radio long before he saw the van. It flew over the rise and swooped past him like a condor pursuing its doomed prey. He looked up and saw Snoops' frightened face hanging out of the rear window. Her brown hair was flying wildly in the wind like the mane of a galloping stallion. "SNOOPS!"

"JEFFER! HELP!"

"I'm comin', Snoops! I'm comin'!" A quarter mile down Route 127 the van made a screeching right turn onto a gravel road. "Dinkus, how far back are you?"

"Not far. I can see you!"

Jeffer glanced back over his shoulder and saw Dinkus coasting down the rise. "The van just turned right onto Howling Wolf Road. Over," said Jeffer. Walnut-sized gravel made it difficult to steer and he had to keep his eyes focused on the road. Every time he glanced up, the van was smaller. "I'm losin' him! Jesus, please help me! I've gotta rescue Snoops!" His legs felt weak and floppy like wet noodles, but he kept pedaling. The next time he looked up, the van had disappeared. Jeffer pulled off to the side of the road to catch his breath. He heard the crunch of gravel and turned to see Dinkus coming up behind him.

"Boy, am I glad to see you," said Dinkus, panting heavily. "I thought I'd never catch up!" He stopped beside Jeffer and wiped the sweat from his grimy face. The shade of the overhanging pine trees and a slight breeze helped the boys cool off.

After a few minutes, Jeffer said, "I'm ready to go on if you are, Dink."

"I'm ready." They pushed off and resumed pedaling.

* * *

"Uh-oh," said Jeffer, slowing to a stop. "We've got a problem."

"I see what you mean," said Dinkus, rolling up beside him. There it was—the last thing Jeffer and Dinkus wanted to see—a fork in the road! "Now what're we gonna do?"

"I don't know," said Jeffer, frowning and scratching his head. "The gravel road to the right continues on through Indian Gap."

"And the dirt road to the left? Where does it go?"

"To only one place," said Jeffer with a worried look on his face. "Straight to Wolf Rocks!"

"WOLF ROCKS! That's where Old Dead Red and his descendants are!"

"I know," said Jeffer gravely. "Let's look closer and see if there are any fresh tire tracks." The boys parked their bikes in the grass and trudged over to where the roads intersected. "It's hard to tell in the gravel," said Jeffer. "And there are several sets of tracks on the dirt road."

"Maybe we should split up," said Dinkus.

"Maybe," said Jeffer, "and maybe not!" He scurried over to examine something lying in the dirt road that had caught his eye. He grinned and said, "Way to go, Snoops!"

"What is it?" asked Dinkus as he joined Jeffer. He looked down and started laughing. "CHEERIOS!"

"Snoops and the dognapper are headed to Wolf Rocks!" said Jeffer.

"Let's go!" said Dinkus.

"No," said Jeffer. "I think you should ride back to The Red Wolf Café and call Sheriff Logan. Tell him that the dognapper has Snoops and that he's holed up out at Wolf Rocks."

"What are *you* gonna do?"

"I'll follow the dirt road and try to find Snoops."

"How are you gonna do that?" said Dinkus. "There are a gazillion places to hide out there!"

"Oh, I've got an idea," said Jeffer with a twinkle in his eye. He hopped on his bike and continued down the dirt road while Dinkus turned around and began pedaling back to Route 127.

* * *

The rutted dirt road violently jostled the van, causing Snoops to lose her balance and fall on the hard floor. She slithered on her stomach back to the dividing wall between the cab and the cargo area. She found a space between the wall and Caleb's cage and squeezed herself in. She grimaced and scrunched up her nose. "Blech! It smells nasty in here! Worse than moldy cheese stuffed into Dinkus' old sneakers!" The foul odor churned her stomach, so she pinched her nostrils shut with her thumb and index finger. "Oh, Caleb," said Snoops, crying, "I'm so glad I found you, but I th-th-think I'm in b-b-big trouble!" There was a heavy padlock on the cage door, so she reached through the wire to scratch him behind his ears. Caleb poked his furry muzzle through the bars and licked her tear-streaked face. "Well, at least we're in this together!"

"ARF!" barked Muttley from the other side of the van.

"And Muttley, too!" said Snoops. She tucked her knobby knees up under her quivering chin and whimpered. "Lord Jesus, p-p-please let Jeffer see the p-p-pile of Cheerios I dropped in the road. Please!"

The vehicle slowed down and began pitching wildly to and fro as it rolled over coconut-sized rocks. Snoops clung tightly to the side of Caleb's cage in order to keep from sliding out into the center of the van again. The pitching gradually ceased and the van coasted silently into a deep sheltered cleft in the massive rock formation known as Wolf Rocks. When the van came to a stop, Snoops sprang out of her hiding place and pulled herself up to the rear window. She squeezed through head first like toothpaste out of a tube and landed in a heap on the moist leaf-strewn ground. She scrambled to her feet and turned to run—straight into the iron grip of the dognapper!

CHAPTER EIGHT

"TARP WILBUR!" said Snoops. "*Y-Y-You're* the dognapper?"

Tarp tightened his hold on her wrists, leaned down to peer into her frightened eyes, and said proudly, "I sure am! And what're *you* gonna do about it?"

"Well, I... I... uhhh," stammered Snoops.

"That's right," said Tarp, "nothin'... because there's nothin' you *can* do."

Snoops twisted her scrawny arms around, trying to wrench free from his vice-like grip. "LET GO OF ME!" she shrieked. "LET GO!" Tarp squeezed harder and dragged her back into Red Wolf Cave. Snoops thrashed about wildly like a flounder on the riverbank, but he was too strong. He tossed her over his shoulder like a sack of turnips and carried her to the rear of the cave. It was dark and damp and smelled like wet dog and mushrooms. He shoved her into an Irish setter-sized dog cage and latched it with a rusty lock.

"Yell and scream all you want," said Tarp. "No one will ever hear you." He turned and grabbed a kerosene lantern from the top of a boulder next to her wire prison. He fumbled with a lighter that he had taken out of his shirt pocket, lit the fabric wick, and placed the lantern back on the flat surface of the rock.

"What're ya g-g-gonna do with m-m-me?" asked Snoops. "You can't keep me in here f-f-forever, y' know."

"I KNOW!" yelled Tarp. He was pacing back and forth like a nervous hyena and running his hands through his greasy hair. He took a deep breath and said, "Right now all I need is to keep you outta my way while I take care of business." He shuffled out to the van and began unloading the dog-filled cages... 24 in all! He toted them in one at a time and released the dogs into a fenced-in area at the very back of the cave.

"Look! There's Schultz... and Ruffles... and Binkie!" said Snoops. "They're all here... even Toodles and Doodles!" Snoops' excitement at finding all of the stolen pets faded as fast as a new pair of jeans. "I've found them, but *now* what? I'm stuck here in this stupid cage." She gasped and her chin dropped to the ground. "*I've been dognapped, too!*"

* * *

As the dirt road neared the foot of the Shadow Ridge Mountains, it narrowed and became rockier. It wound its way around moss-covered boulders and through lush fern-filled gullies.

"I must be gettin' close to Wolf Rocks," said Jeffer, struggling to keep his bike upright. As he maneuvered around a huge rock the size of a Volkswagen, his front tire hit a deep rut. He sailed over the handle-bars with arms out-stretched like a flying squirrel and landed on his face in a fern patch. "Thlipppph!" He spat out fragments of fern fronds and wiped smudges of rich dark earth from his face. "This bike's not cuttin' it anymore." He pushed it over to the nearest tree and leaned it up against the gnarled trunk. With the heel of his sneaker he traced an arrow that pointed toward Wolf Rocks in the soft dirt. "When Sheriff Logan sees this, he'll know where I'm headed."

Jeffer made good time on foot, jogging when the terrain permitted. He stumbled down a small hill, rounded a curve, and came to a screeching halt. "Oh, no! *Another* fork in the road!" Only this time there were no Cheerios to guide him and the trail was too rocky to show any evidence of recent tire tracks. "Dear Lord, what am I gonna do? Which way should I go?" He gazed skyward, almost hoping to hear an audible "Go right!" or "Go left!" shouted from the heavens. He sized up the trail to the left; he sized up the trail to the right. "Well," said Jeffer, "whichever way I choose, I've got a 50-50 chance of being correct." He rubbed his chin... and rubbed it some more. "If I'm wrong, I can always come back and take the other path." He rubbed his chin one more time and said, "Last time I went left, so this time I'll go right." He foraged around and found three thick sticks—one long and two short—and laid them on the ground in the shape of an arrow pointing to the trail on the right.

It wasn't long before Jeffer realized that the path he had picked was going steadily uphill. When he reached a point where he had to climb more than walk, he knew he had chosen incorrectly. "There's no way that the dognapper's van could go very far on this trail. I'm gonna have to go back." He turned to go, but then paused to think. "If this trail continues on up to the very top of Wolf Rocks, then it might be worth the trip. I'll be able to look all around. Maybe I'll even see Snoops and the van." He imagined Dinkus adding, "Yeah, and maybe you'll see old Dead Red, too!"

* * *

"WOW! This is amazing!" said Jeffer, standing on the summit of Wolf Rocks and drinking in the view before him. The flat stone surface of the giant rock formation stretched out to his right. Beyond, as far as his brown eyes could see, were the forest-covered peaks and valleys of the Shadow Ridge Mountains. "This would be a great place to camp... if it weren't for the wolves... and the dognapper!"

He hiked to the far edge of the stone table-top, leaping over several two-foot wide crevices as he went. These wide cracks between the massive rocks were 50 to 60 feet deep. Jeffer tried not to think about that. He cautiously approached the rocky rim. After securing his footing, he leaned out and looked down... way down. He stood silently like a stone sentinel and watched for several minutes, hoping to see some kind of unusual activity below that might help him locate Snoops and the dognapper. "There's nothin' goin' on down there," said Jeffer, shaking his head, "at least not that I can see."

He turned and was heading back to the trailhead when something in the waist-high brush to his left caught his eye. He crept closer, hoping to get a better look... and hoping that it was not Old Dead Red. "A couple more steps and I think I'll be able to see what it is." He inched his way to within six feet of the object. "It looks like something hidden under a piece of green canvas," he said, relieved that it was not 180 pounds of snarling, growling ferociousness. He grabbed hold of one end of the rough canvas and yanked it back as hard as he could. It got hung up, so he leaned back and tugged even harder. The tarp flew off and landed in a heap at Jeffer's feet.

"AHHHHHH!" he hollered. The hair on his head stood straight up and his eyes bulged wide with fright. "IT'S OLD DEAD RED!" His feet were frozen to the ground, so he just stood there, staring at the huge hairy wolf. Old Dead Red stared back... and kept staring... and staring. He didn't even blink! Not a muscle twitched. Not even a flick of his tail. "It doesn't even look like he's breathing," whispered Jeffer. He gazed intently at the ferocious furry fiend. A wide grin slowly spread across his face. "He doesn't look like he's breathing," he said, "because he's *not!*" He strolled right up to the wolf and patted him on the head. "He's stuffed!"

Jeffer carefully examined the taxidermy wolf. He was mounted in a sitting position on a square wooden base, which had four wheels underneath. Next to the rolling wolf was a large loudspeaker and a CD player, both hooked up to a portable gas-powered inverter generator. "I'll bet the dognapper's been using Old Really Dead Red here to scare folks away from Wolf Rocks and his hideout. He probably rolls Mr. Wolf out to the edge where his silhouette can be seen in the moonlight and then he cranks up the howling wolf CD. Pretty good set-up... and effective, too. Nobody's been out here for months... not since the rumors about the return of Old Dead Red's descendants started circulating." He tossed the canvas back over the loudspeaker, CD player, generator, and wolf and started down the mountain. "I'll bring

Sheriff Logan up here later," said Jeffer, "but right now I've gotta find Snoops!"

* * *

At the fork in the trail, Jeffer picked up the three sticks and placed them back in arrow formation, this time pointing toward the path on the left. "I sure hope Dinkus was able to get hold of Sheriff Logan. I think I'm gonna need his help real soon."

This trail was wider than the other one and Jeffer was able to cover distance quickly. It sloped gently downhill and, after curving around several large boulders, ran the length of Wolf Rocks at the base of the formation. "Somewhere along here is Red Wolf Cave," said Jeffer. "I'll bet that's where the dognapper's hiding out... with Snoops." He hiked a little further down the path and said, "Now it's time for my secret weapon!" He dug through his jeans pocket until he found it... the shiny silver dog whistle.

CHAPTER NINE

"**A**RF! ARF! WOOF! YAP-YAP-YAP!" The sound of 24 caroling canines flooded the cave and ricocheted off of the cold stone walls.

"What's gotten into these mutts?" said Tarp. "All this barking is driving me nuts!"

Snoops clamped her hands over her ears and smiled. She no longer wondered what good a whistle was that couldn't be heard!

"What are *you* so happy about?" Tarp said sharply.

Snoops abruptly stopped grinning and said, "Who... m-m-me?"

"Yeah, you. Who else would I be talkin' to?"

"I dunno... maybe to one of the dogs you stole!" said Snoops boldly.

"It's no big deal," said Tarp. "They're just dogs."

"They're not just dogs. They're people's pets! They love them and want 'em back."

"Too bad... they're mine now and I'll do whatever I want to with 'em."

"Just because you stole them, doesn't make 'em yours," said Snoops. "Taking something that doesn't belong to you is stealing and God says that stealing's a sin."

"I don't care what God says. All I care about is the money I can make selling these mangy mongrels."

"Does your uncle know that you're a thief?" asked Snoops.

Tarp threw back his head and cackled wickedly. His maniacal laughter was interrupted by another deafening wave of howling from the penned-up pooches. "SHUT UP!" yelled Tarp as he covered his ears. "I can't take this anymore! I'm going outside 'til they calm down."

* * *

"I hear barking!" said Jeffer. He crept closer to the well-hidden cavern entrance and blew the dog whistle again.

"YAP-YAP! ARF! WOOF-WOOF-WOOF!"

Spying a large, thick shrub by the opening, he dropped to his hands and knees and scuttled behind it. He had just finished concealing himself when an aggravated Tarp Wilbur stomped out of the cave. Jeffer gasped, "Tarp Wilbur!" He quickly covered his mouth with his hand, hoping that he hadn't made too much noise.

Tarp was making too much noise of his own to have heard Jeffer. "Those crazy dogs! Why don't they stop carryin' on? I can't even hear myself think in there!"

Jeffer chuckled and blew the whistle one more time for good measure. Tarp shuffled a little further down the path until he was out of earshot of the melodious mutts.

"Now's my chance!" said Jeffer. He slithered out from under the bush and into the cave. The lantern light cast long shadows on the damp earthen floor. Jeffer's eyes gradually adjusted to the dimly lit stone room. Not knowing if there were any other dognappers still in the cave, he hugged the rough rock wall and hid in the shadows. He spotted a boulder, scurried behind it, and poked his head out on the other side.

"Psssst! Hey, Snoops!"

Snoops whirled around. "Jeffer! I knew you'd find me. I just knew it!"

"What kind of mess have you gotten yourself into this time?" said Jeffer, eyeing her padlocked prison.

"I'm in a bit of a jam," said Snoops.

"I'll say! I can't believe that the dognapper is Tarp Wilbur!"

"Me, neither," said Snoops. "He always seemed so harmless and quiet... like a marshmallow."

"Is he the only one?"

"As far as I know," said Snoops. "I haven't seen anyone else."

Jeffer looked at Snoops trapped in the cage and shook his head. "What in the world were you thinkin' when you climbed into that van, Snoops?"

Snoops' lower lip quivered like cherry red Jell-O and she started crying. "I wasn't thinking at all! I just wanted to be with Caleb." She was almost sobbing now. "I'm scared, Jeffer. I really, *really* need a 'fear not' verse!"

Jeffer rubbed his chin and thought. "Hmmm... how 'bout this one? 'In God I have put my trust; I shall not be afraid. What can mere man do to me?'"

"That's a good one," said Snoops, sniffling and wiping her tears away.

"God's bigger and stronger than puny ol' Tarp Wilbur," said Jeffer, "and He'll help me get you outta here."

"Where's Dinkus?"

"I sent him back to The Red Wolf Café to call Sheriff Logan."

"I feel better knowing that he's on the way," said Snoops.

"Me, too," said Jeffer, "but we don't know how long it'll take for him to get here. So in the meantime, let's figure out how to get you out of this cage." He inspected the rusty lock and all the hinges and joints. "You wouldn't happen to have a pair of wire cutters on you, would ya?"

"No, I left them at home along with my laser cannon and light saber," said Snoops dryly.

"Well, at least you haven't lost your sense of humor!" said Jeffer as he peered more closely at one of the corner joints. "What I really need is a screwdriver."

"Flathead or Phillips?" asked Snoops.

Jeffer gazed at her in disbelief, his mouth hanging open.

"What?" said Snoops. "Can't a girl know about tools, too?"

"Sure," said Jeffer slowly. "So?"

"So what?"

"So... do you have a screwdriver?"

"Which kind?" said Snoops. "You still haven't told me."

"Uhm... flathead," said Jeffer.

"No, I don't have one of those."

"Do you have *any* tools in that overall bib pocket of yours?" asked Jeffer.

"No," said Snoops. "But I might have somethin' that'll work just as good." She unsnapped the pocket and rooted around inside. "Remember that strawberry gumball I wanted to get out of the machine in front of the pharmacy?"

"Yeah," said Jeffer, "but what does that have to do with anything?"

"Well," said Snoops, "I never got the gumball. We stopped to talk to Josh about Fuzzball and I forgot all about it."

"So what?"

"Since I didn't get the gumball, I still have the dime!" said Snoops, pulling the shiny coin out of her pocket.

Jeffer's eyes lit up. "We can use that dime as a makeshift flathead screwdriver!"

"Exactly!" said Snoops.

"The screws are a bit rusty," said Jeffer, "but I think it'll work. If I can remove the screws from all four corners, then the back side of the cage should come off." He grasped the coin between his thumb and index finger, slid it into the narrow slot on the head of the metal screw, and twisted it. It didn't budge. "It's really stuck, Snoops."

"Keep trying," said Snoops. "You've *got* to get me outta here!"

"OK," said Jeffer, "here it goes." He tried to turn the screw again, putting every ounce of strength he had behind it. The extreme effort caused his face to contort into an ugly grimace.

Snoops giggled. "You're making that scrunched-up gopher face you make whenever Doc Watkins gives you a shot."

Jeffer ignored her and kept on straining. "It's loosening up! I think it turned a little." With each slow and painful twist of his wrist, the rusty screw gradually loosened to the point that Jeffer could use just his fingers to turn it and eventually pull it out. "One down... three more to go."

"Hurry, Jeffer, hurry!"

"I'm hurryin' as fast as I can," said Jeffer, "but it's slow going."

"I think I hear Tarp coming back!" said Snoops. Jeffer ducked behind the boulder just as Tarp trudged in.

"I thought I heard voices in here," said Tarp, standing in front of Snoops' cage. "Who were ya talkin' to just now?"

"Well, I... uh... uh... I was just talking to the dogs," said Snoops. "Yep... just talkin' to the dogs."

BEEP-BEEP! BEEP-BEEP! The sound of a car horn cut through the air and echoed in the hollow cavern.

"Is it 5:00 already?" said Tarp, glancing at his watch. He trotted out of the cave to meet his fellow dognapper.

"Is he gone?" whispered Jeffer.

"Yeah, he's gone," said Snoops. "You can come out now."

Jeffer scooted out from his hiding place. "Whew! That was a close one." He picked up the dime and got back to work.

"I'll say," said Snoops. "And now there's someone else here, too!"

"So I heard."

"You don't seem surprised."

"I'm not," said Jeffer. "After what I discovered up on top of Wolf Rocks, I sort of figured that Tarp Wilbur wasn't smart enough to pull off this kind of a scheme all by himself."

"After what you discovered? What exactly did you find up there?" asked Snoops.

"A loudspeaker, a CD player, a generator, and... Old Really Dead Red."

"OLD DEAD RED?!"

"No," said Jeffer, "Old *Really* Dead Red... a taxidermy wolf."

"A taxigermy wolf?" said Snoops.

"No, not taxi*germ*y... taxi*derm*y," said Jeffer, "as in stuffed."

"A stuffed Old Dead Red?" said Snoops. "I don't understand, Jeffer."

"I'll tell ya more about it later. Right now let's concentrate on loosening these screws, OK?"

"How many more to go?"

"Two more... no, make that one more," said Jeffer, pulling out the third screw.

"Once you get me outta here, what's the plan?"

"Well..."

"You *do* have a plan, don't you, Jeffer?"

"Ummm... not yet."

"NOT YET?" said Snoops, her eyes popping out of their sockets.

"Don't worry. I'll come up with somethin'," said Jeffer confidently.

Snoops tilted her head to one side and listened, hoping to hear the gears turning in his head. "Sounds more like hamster wheels to me," she mumbled. "How ya comin' with that last screw?"

"Almost there."

"Good," said Snoops. "I can hardly wait to get outta here!"

"Actually," said Jeffer, "you need to stay in there just a little while longer."

"*What?*" said Snoops. "Why?"

"Because Tarp and the other creep are gonna be comin' back in here any second now and it's got to look like everything's the way it was," said Jeffer. "I've got an idea, but we need the element of surprise." He removed the last screw and shook the back panel free. "OK, Snoops. The back of the cage is loose. It's just leaning up against the sides, so be careful not to move around too much."

"How will I know when to break out?"

"Trust me," said Jeffer with a gleam in his eye, "you'll know."

CHAPTER TEN

"**R**emember to wait for my signal, Snoops," whispered Jeffer from behind a large jagged rock on the other side of the cavern.

"OK." She shook her head and said, "Why I let myself get caught up in your crazy ideas I'll never know." As harebrained as his schemes were, Snoops took comfort in the fact that they usually worked!

"I think you got *yourself* caught up this time," said Jeffer. "You're the one sittin' in a cage, not me!"

"True... how very true," said Snoops, peering out at him from behind the metal bars.

"Shhhhhh!" said Jeffer with his index finger to his lips. "I think I hear voices!"

"Inside your head or outside?"

Jeffer turned and glared at her. "Not *in* my head, silly! Outside and comin' this way!" He ducked back down behind the boulder.

The voices came closer. "Don't worry, Tarp. Everything's going to be just fine. After we get rid of the Culverton dogs, we'll lay low for a while... until the heat's off."

"That voice sounds familiar," thought Jeffer, "but I can't quite place it."

"Speaking of h-h-heat," stammered Tarp, "there's something I need to t-t-tell you."

"What is so urgent that it can't wait until later?"

"Follow me and I'll show you," said Tarp. They entered the lantern-lit room. "I had a little trouble this afternoon."

"What kind of trouble?"

"Well... uh... it's hard to explain."

"Try anyway!" said the man, his voice getting louder.

"It might be easier if you see for yourself."

"See what?"

"Over there... in that cage," said Tarp, pointing at Snoops.

The second dognapper took one look at Snoops huddled in the corner of the cage and hollered, "TARP! WHAT HAVE YOU DONE?"

Snoops took one look at the man and yelled, "MR. P-P-PEERSON! YOU'RE A D-D-DOGNAPPER?"

Upon hearing Snoops call out Mr. Peerson's name, a sharp dagger of betrayal pierced through Jeffer's tender heart and he began to cry. He hunkered down behind the rock and bit his lower lip, trying to control his emotions.

"WHAT IN THE WORLD WERE YOU THINKING, TARP?" screamed Mr. Peerson. "Do you have any idea what you've done?"

"She was hiding in the van," said Tarp. "I couldn't let her go. She would've gone straight to the sheriff."

"You really don't get it, do you?"

"Get what, Uncle Milt?"

"By keeping her against her will you became guilty of kidnapping!"

"KIDNAPPING?" said Tarp in disbelief.

"Yes!" said Mr. Peerson. "Stealing dogs is one thing, but kidnapping is quite another!"

"And if you don't let me outta this cage right now, then you're a kidnapper, too!" said Snoops to Mr. Peerson, giving him the hairy eyeball for added effect.

"What're we gonna do?" said Tarp, panic rising in his voice. "I don't wanna go to jail!"

"You should've thought of that before you stole Winston," said Snoops.

"Who's Winston?" asked Tarp.

"Winston the bulldog," said Snoops, "the first dog you snatched."

"Tarp, stop talking to her and help me pack up!" said Mr. Peerson. "We need to get out of here *now*!"

"YOU'RE NOT GOIN' ANYWHERE!" yelled Jeffer as he sprang up like a jack-in-the-box from his hiding place. Snoops burst out of the back of her cage and they dashed over to the fenced-in area. Jeffer threw open the gate and hollered, "RELEASE THE HOUNDS!" Twenty-four yelping, yapping dogs surged like a tidal wave through the gate toward their abductors. Mr. Peerson and Tarp screamed like little girls on a roller coaster. They turned to bolt, but instead were pinned up against the rough stone wall by the pack of agitated animals.

"Down, boys, down!" commanded Jeffer. "Sit!" The dogs sat, but continued to bark and howl at Tarp and Mr. Peerson.

Jeffer stared at Mr. Peerson, tears of betrayal still stinging his eyes. "Mr. Peerson, how could you do this? I thought you were our friend. I thought you loved animals!"

"I do love animals, Jeffer," said Mr. Peerson.

"No, you don't," said Snoops angrily. "If you loved them, you wouldn't take 'em away from their families. YOU STOLE OUR CALEB! AND DINKUS' MUTTLEY! You don't love them at all... you only love yourself!" She folded her arms across her chest and scowled at the two dognappers.

"So Snoops, what do ya think we should do with these two crooks?" said Jeffer. "Let the dogs gnaw on their bones?"

"No," said Snoops, "I have a better idea!"

* * *

"JEFFER! SNOOPS! Where are you?" a voice called from outside the cavern.

"That sounds like Dinkus!" said Jeffer.

"WE'RE IN HERE!" yelled Snoops. Moments later Dinkus burst into the cave, followed by Sheriff Logan.

"Boy, are we glad to see you guys!" said Jeffer, slapping Dinkus on the back.

"Not half as glad as we are to see that you two are OK," said Sheriff Logan. "Especially you, Rebecca. When Dinkus told me what had happened... well, let's just say that I was very concerned. What in the world were you thinking?"

"That seems to be the question of the day," sighed Snoops, "and all I can say is that I wasn't thinking at all... and I'm so sorry."

Sheriff Logan wrapped his strong arm around her small shoulders. "All is forgiven... but don't you *ever* do anything like that EVER AGAIN!" His booming voice startled her, but she knew that he was upset because he cared about her. "I'm sure that your parents will be discussing the matter with you as well."

"Yes, I'm sure they will," said Snoops solemnly, dreading the prospect of explaining herself and her lack of thought yet again.

"Jeffer," said Sheriff Logan, "I saw the dognappers' car and van and I can see that you and Snoops are safe... but where are the dognappers themselves?"

"Over there," said Jeffer, pointing to a collie-sized cage across the room. Tarp and Mr. Peerson were crammed into the small space with their knees tucked up to their chins. The pack of purloined pooches encircled their wire prison, glaring at them and occasionally barking to keep them quiet. "It was Snoops' idea to stick 'em in there."

"Let's just call it payback," said Snoops. Sheriff Logan and Dinkus stepped forward to get a better look at the dognappers.

"TARP WILBUR!" said Dinkus.

"AND MILT PEERSON!" added the sheriff. "You're responsible for all the dognappings in Culverton?" Sheriff Logan removed his hat and scratched his head. "Never in a million years would I have suspected you two... especially you, Milt." He put his hat back on and shook his head in disbelief and disappointment.

"What'll we do now, Sheriff?" said Jeffer.

Sheriff Logan surveyed the room, drinking it all in. "Let's see... two caged dognappers, two impounded vehicles, three brave children, and 24 stolen dogs... I think I'll call for backup!"

* * *

"Double bacon cheeseburgers all around!" Sheriff Logan called out to Maggie and Pete. "With fries!" He was perched on a stool at the counter in The Red Wolf Café along with Jeffer, Snoops, Dinkus, Mr. and Mrs. Malone, and Mr. and Mrs. Elliott. "Raise your glasses with me," he said as he hoisted his chocolate milkshake into the air. "Here's to the three best junior detectives this side of the Mississippi!"

"Here! Here!" said everybody, followed by the clinking of glasses and light-hearted laughter.

"Did you see Josh's face yesterday when he was reunited with Fuzzball?" said Dinkus. "That was priceless!"

"It was crazy out there in the café parking lot last night!" said Jeffer. "Twenty-four tail-waggin' pooches and their happy owners huggin' and slobberin' all over each other!"

"Yeah," said Snoops, "and everybody was laughing and bawling all at the same time."

"You included," said Dinkus.

"I know," said Snoops, "wasn't it great?" She stirred her vanilla shake with a red plastic straw and took a long, slow sip. "Mmm-mmm...this sure tastes a whole lot better than stale Cheerios from the bottom of my overall bib pocket!"

"Say, Sheriff," said Maggie, "what's going to happen to Milt Peerson and Tarp Wilbur?"

"Do you know what they'll be charged with?" asked Pete.

"How 'bout Grand Theft Fido and Snoops-napping?" said Dinkus.

Sheriff Logan chuckled and said, "Seriously, those two are facing some heavy charges... kidnapping, confinement, and felony theft."

"Those are serious crimes," said Mr. Malone.

"Yes, they are," said the sheriff. "They'll both be in prison for a very long time."

"That's a high price to pay for dognapping," said Jeffer.

"Hey!" said Snoops. "Don't forget, they dognapped me, too!"

"Snoops," said Dinkus, "you're not a dog, so you couldn't have been *dog*napped."

"Yeah," said Jeffer, "you're a kid. You were *kid*napped."

"Kidnapped or dognapped," said Snoops. "What difference does it make? All I know is that I was 'napped and stuffed into a cage like a pimento into an olive!"

"Sheriff," said Mr. Elliott, "did you find the wolf and the generator that Jeffer discovered on top of Wolf Rocks?"

"We sure did. I sent Deputy Meeks up there this morning. He and another officer brought down all the equipment and put it in the evidence locker at the station."

"That was some set-up with the taxidermy wolf and the CD player with the loud speaker, wasn't it?" said Jeffer.

"It sure was," said the sheriff. "It kept people away from Wolf Rocks for months while Tarp and Milt ran their dognapping operation."

"Hey!" said Pete Halverson. "You kids *are* good detectives! You not only solved the dognapping mystery, but you also solved the mystery of the return of Old Dead Red!"

"I think you mean Old *Really* Dead Red," said Jeffer.

"That's right," said Dinkus. "You can't get much deader than being dead and stuffed!"

Maggie came out from the kitchen carrying platters of juicy sizzling bacon burgers and hot crispy fries. She set a plate down in front of each customer and brought several bottles of ketchup and extra napkins.

"Who wants to bless the food?" said Mr. Elliott.

"I do!" said Dinkus. He folded his hands and bowed his head. "Dear Lord, thank You so much for helping us find Snoops and all the missing dogs... especially Caleb and Muttley. And thank You for these burgers and fries. In Jesus' name, amen."

"Amen. EVERYBODY DIG IN!" said Sheriff Logan. "Lunch is on me!"

"Lunch isn't on *you*," said Snoops. "It's on the counter."

"'On me' means I'm paying for it."

"Really?" said Snoops. "Thank you!"

"Yes... thank you!" said everyone else at the counter.

"It's the least I can do for my three favorite sleuths and their parents," said Sheriff Logan.

Dinkus chomped down on his ketch-up-dripping sandwich and said with his mouth full, "Eat up, Snoops! These beefy bacon burgers are good for helping us keep up our strength."

"Why do we need to keep up our strength?" asked Snoops.

"I know why!" said Jeffer with a twinkle in his eye. "So we're ready to tackle our next mystery, of course!"

"I wonder when that will be," said Snoops, nibbling on a fry.

"NOT SOON ENOUGH!" said Jeffer and Dinkus.

CPSIA information can be obtained
at www.ICGtesting.com
Printed in the USA
LVOW10s0919300817
546868LV00014B/99/P